Beloved

A Compilation of Love Poems

Caroline Parajo

BookLeaf
Publishing
India | USA | UK

Presentation by *BookLeaf Publishing*

Web: www.bookleafpub.com

E-mail: info@bookleafpub.com

ISBN: 9789363315112

First edition 2024

Strong suit

maybe strong words weren't my best suit

and i never, ever failed to

commit to write my wrongs for you

for my love is strong and true

no matter how regretful one becomes

it is worth noting

Meeting you was fate

Meeting you was fate

Remaining friends was a choice

I'd stare and speak to you everyday

But I've done not enough

to even sit and drink alone and think

of you on lonely days

What's a girl gotta do

for you

to stay?

'Cause it was beyond my control

to even fall

in love with you in every way

What's a girl gotta do

to stay

for you?

Love at first sight

We try to hide our feelings, but we forget our eyes speak.

We tell each other's favourites, but your telling eyes make me weak.

Woke up with these lines

5

Our heads lay on separate pillows

Our thoughts drift into guilt pleasures

Our bodies lay on separate beds

Our eyes are both still seeking treasures

Blue skies

I got heart eyes for you

Lost in your hazy hue

Oh what a beautiful view

When lying next to you

To wake up by your side

Is where I wanna be right

And not after the sunrise

All I wanna see is your blue skies

My eyes will seek only you

My heart longs for you

Oh when love birds come in two's

They sing their paired songs in tune

Lower your drawn bow it would do

Like feet fit the perfect shoe

Uplifted nights sway for you

And not a day goes by

Without clouds thinking to cry

You pulled me into your blue skies

It's with you

it's with you,

that i don't wanna ruin

a beautiful and good thing

'cause we started off

at the right turn

and it's become like a slow burn,

it's got me overthinking

or could be just me without thinking,

i gave in to a new sensation

now i'm just a fool to rush in

to the passion that can never see me leaving,

some sprint for just a fling

others wait for the one to buy a ring

i'd say, it's with you,

you're the one in my life that's been missing

unlike me, i'd come back for that one last song to
sing

but you stayed like the first sunray

that touches and misses one's skin

and as the first message that wakes the morning

i say a little prayer, kneeling

for nothing more than to ask when can i

feel a thousand more feelings with you

Winnin' at life

i want all my dreams
to be about you
when I sleep
i'm livin' for you,

'cause when I'm with you
i'm winnin' at life
even before my past life
i look forward to time with you

traced along paths
the map i followed to
was steps to your heart
drawn with permanent marks

Map Of Us

It could be

So romantic

To sail the

Whole Atlantic, with you

We can just forget about the world,

And explore that mind of yours

We could run

Away to somewhere beautiful

But I want

To stay

And explore that mind of yours

Forget where we belong,

Forgive me, I'm still young

You gave yourself

All your shadows and layers

You read me so well

I let you turn my pages

Shared my hopes, dreams and fears

I never knew before

I could ride

the waves of The Titanic

By your side but

Love is so tragic, with you

Cause you'd say "just forget about me girl

Go perform that life of yours"

But I jumped, yeah I fell

In the sea to carry your boat

This shipwreck of tears will

Drown in what we wrote

'Cause I could play

the acoustic of music

Sheet notes all translucent

Fingers know it all so fluently

All the things that used to hurt,

Don't anymore

When you are my world, and I am yours

I wonder why

I circle back to you

Just like the map of us you drew

In your palm, yeah you know it like the back of
your hand

Traced along my heart, I can

Draw a map to yours

Cause I'm drawn to you, yeah, I follow it like the
traces of your back

I guess you're floating away

Slipping through my fingers

I see you sailing away

Feelings for you still linger

All the feelings that would hurt, don't anymore

Can you draw me a map to you?

'Cause you are my world, and I am yours

Can you draw a map of us

We're in a world of our own

Lucky love

I knew it was luck

When I found my ladybug,

He gardens my love

How it was so far-flung

I never thought

I'd be stuck in your painted love

'Cause I could say, you're a work of art

I never met

Anyone like you from a frameless past

Did I find my happy ever after?

'Cause eyes found a four-leaf clover

One hand plucked, feet almost stepped over,

Couldn't help but wonder,

To count the petals

Now I can't get over you,

My lucky love

To one's heart's content

you are my heaven

but here on earth

you love me like i'm of well worth

you are so encouraging

when giving compliments

it makes me feel feminine

you are beauty

you are depth

love me like it's your first breath

i feel so lucky

you fill my heart's content

you are my calm energy

You

you were my muse

my daydream

my Paris

and of all the places i've been to,

your arms seem to be my favourite one

you were my light

my gravity

my wonderland

and of all the days i'm with you,

it feels like a holiday

Speak my love language

no matter if you scream

loud storms in my soul

you would still calm me

for when i'd breathe

you still leave me breathless,

yet never was it known,

you'd sing goose bumps to me

and whispers to my heart

all in all,

you spoke my love language at best

Happy place

you're a viewer

more than a reader,

less of a teller

more of a keeper

i found love

you would fight

more than defend,

and rather dive

into the deep end

in the waters

we call love

i know a place to slay all your demons

lay with me

all your problems and your worries

oh i just want you to be happy

i get drunk on your honesty

i know any place can be happy

as long as you're with me

i wanna remember you like a daydream

we can forget all the nightmares that are
happening

Loved by an angel

They say old ways won't open new doors

But this is my way of saying I could soar

They say the old days were better than before,
than it is now

But these days I rise to what brings me down

If my wings, exist, to fly

If I get there, in time

We won't fall

And we won't fail

In our troubles that catch up to us,

Cause we are angels, still,

No we won't go

And we won't sail

In the tears that come down to drown us

I lean on your hands that you lend

Cause we are angels, angels in the end

They say to give up the dream, you give in to the
work

'Cause every time I look at the stars, I fall into
the dirt

They say you've got to hold onto time and let
her heal ya

But just listen to your heart, she's the best
preacher

She'll say my wings exist to fly

If I get there in time, I will fly

We won't fall

And we won't fail

In our troubles that catch up to us,

No we won't go

We won't sail

In the tears that come down to drown us

Cause we are angels by the end

Still angels

And if my wings exist to fly

I lean on your hands that you lend

Keep these wings stable tonight

Keep this love if I have the will to try

To adjust the currents in notable time

And I am loved by an angel

Wild fire

you were a wild fire

set to my heart

and we're never gonna die

from what we had at the start

i'm never gonna stop writing

'bout what we were, and what we now aren't

just to keep the flame living on

the more times i think about you

and most nights i wonder if you ever think about
me too

chasing each other's shadow

we can't seem to let go

you keep up with the follow

i'm trying to hate you, oh,

you were a wild fire

set to my heart

and we're never gonna die

from what we had at the start

i'm never gonna stop writing

'bout what we were, and what we now aren't

just to keep the flame living on

Funny little thing

there's a funny little thing called love

flower fields no way amount to what one wants

here's a daily dose of do's and dont's

scripted scenes never play out to what i wrote

cheers to films for making old love seem real for
young ones

I'm not your type

But who would've thought that

I'd be looking for somebody like you

And you'd be looking for me too

I'm not your prize

I'm just a small package

Filled with surprises

And you're the only one I'd open up to

Beautifully Unreachable

'Cause you made me beautiful among a million stars

And I keep asking myself what had teared us apart

And I know I can't have you

'Cause you're untouchable

'Cause you're the type to fall in love with the moon

So beautifully unreachable

I loved you from the very start

And still love you from afar

'Cause you have my heart

Date night

I got my hair tied, nails filed

He got me tongue-tied, will sparks fly?

With my jeans skin tight, should I go for a
smoky eye?

He got that perfect smile and deep brown eyes

Boy, do you remember our first date night?

An hour late,

waited 'til eight before you arrived

Outside my home, with the Christmas lights on,

Hoping by the end of the night,

You'd know the stars would align for the both of
us, tonight but i'm

Re-discovering our fate underneath a bed of a
thousand stars

Oh replaying our date over in my head it's gone
a little too far

Into thinking that we could still be a lovely pair,

Why didn't I know

That this would be unfair

The first of many,

Lies

Oh, I swear

Why did I care

That this would be

The first of many

lies,

That I'm aware

I'm aware

Oh, asking why,

Too many times that you would fool me?

Asking why'd, I left behind,

Too many lovers so you could kiss me?

We had those late nights, the stayed-up kinds

We had those talks that turned later to fights

You left me love bites, in the back seat of your
ride

Fast forward to -last night, kicked me out to the
kerb side

Do you remember the other date we had
planned?

So out cold,

Hiding by the boat, where I was standing

Outside your home, while you were out getting
high

Hopes died by the end of the night

You'd know those sparks turned off for the both
of us tonight

Note to self

when all is said and done

no need to pick your poison

'cause that tongue of yours is troublesome

then, you're dead and gone

'cause of death was hoped

all 'cause you drunk on red and smoked for fun

a warm voice tone was your cool undertone

yeah i know we're done, i self note

yeah you weren't the one, but i'm still -

running on your mouth, you're

running on my skin, you

bite me 'til i need, until i need, the antidote,

your hands on me, yet Love hands me

warning notes

so say tomorrow

that we'll both grow

yet i've been throwing dead flowers you gave me

i care 'bout ya' baby,

but better done trying

so spare, the letters

that you've been writing, oh that you wrote,

to save me

i care 'bout ya' baby

but please i'm done waiting

for you to love me

so say tomorrow that we both know

that i've been writing just to save me,

writing just to save me

you left me on read and into your comfort zone

yeah i know we're done, i self note

yeah you weren't the one, but i'm still -

runnin' out of love, you're

runnin' low on chances

'bout to drive to you, but when i step on the gas,
and

i have my hands on my wheel of my car, yet all i
see are

warning signs

Is your love worthy

your love is what i learnt

that cannot be measured for what it's worth

though it was overflowing

love can be hard to handle

and too young to afford it

a day without talking is a waste

a love with you is too good not to erase

the wings of mine, they were once broken

being clipped

the cuts from the knife, they were unequal

being vulnerable

Mmm…

Twisting like liquorice

Were our tasty kisses

Cotton candy

Turned into your sweetened caresses

We're smooth and silky honey

Were your words running dripped in thirst?

'Cause your stare was like how you eyed dessert

Evening kisses

darling,

how you swung out of the blue

i'd forgotten you

those times i snuck out of my room

just to drive and see you

how i long for your evening kisses

we'd fight for no good reason,

how we talked through the morning

saying we'll get through this,

but we left it in pieces

now i cry that i don't see you

completely turn over to the side of the bed

i'm holding by the thread

darling,

how there can't be somebody out there for me,

and nobody can be 'you'

oh how could you not be the one

and i know you more than anyone could

why did i hear from you now

and when you told me that i'll always matter to you,

how you're not here and it's unfair

that i've been missing

your evening kisses

Lightyears

you are lightyears away

but out of all the days, you say 'hey'

why'd the stars align today,

i can't speak out your name,

i'll be outta my mind

i could go insane

going round in circles,

chasing hearts, gowned in purple,

how you leave me painful scars that escape on
my skin you used to trace

but out of all the marks, yours still stays

even if you were lightyears away

yeah out of all the marks, yours truly is left to
stay

even if you were lightyears away

What it feels like to be young

Chewing gum,
'Til the flavours gone
Tantrums sung
'Til it roared eardrums

Blurry night visions
With whiskey and rum
Of origami skies and
Vermicelli white suns

Breathing star-like dust
Clouded ring puffs
The night is still young
Like us, where we are from

This is what it feels
Like to be young,
And dumb
And how high,
Fun it is 'til morning comes

Unbroken

41

You can put oceans between us

But my mind won't stop swimming towards -

You can ignite a fire between us

But I'd still walk through and burn for you

Toxic

And when the flesh burns as we both touch

I knew I was the ocean trying to love

The fire

Waves

43

You are the wave

that rolls in

I feel your way

keep on coming

back to me

And as I see

you almost reach my feet

you then run away

from me

Shall i compare thee to a summer's day?

shall i compare thee to a summer's day?

you've rekindled

all these fireflies

inside of me, hey

candlelit sky was like giving birth

twinkling a sea of stars

like floating paper lanterns

a burnt offering to the night

i've watched millions of sunrises

those fiery skies,

yet could never catch my eye

like you do

a glowing image of you, a sun-kissed you

you're breathtaking beauty

yes, a warm hue looks good on you

and has never been so true

Unfateful

It started with a smile
and ended in tears
I loved you for a while
then it disappeared

It started with a lie
and ended in truth
To tell wrong from right
Was my heart all for use?

Instead used to leave me
with twinkles in my eyes
Now you left me
staring at starless skies

I love you still…

I'm not the one you're missing when you're
kissing me
But I love you still
Even though she's there to steal
Your heart from me
I'm not the one you're dreaming of when you're
sleeping next to me
But I love you still
Even though she's there to steal your heart from
me.

Dumb poem

i know you like

the back of my hand

but i don't like

wasted time i can't get back

i ain't f*cking around

no, i'm not getting any younger

i know i'd be lying,

twiddling them thumbs

of me just writing

another dumb poem

if you move aside

yeah, i promise to move forward

but why does it have to be subliminal

the messages you left, i read them all

and just like a toy, it was shiny and new

so luminous, yet dangerous,

you were just a boy, for all i knew

falling as the stars fall
burning as they do
shining like that, giving their all
that's my love for you

Head over heels

it's like secretly kissing in a Ferris wheel
walking on, stepping into minefields
tiptoeing through, a creaky stairwell
laid me a path of eggshells, for our love is
kinda dangerous
a little courageous
much more frivolous,

and when my head's spinning 'round like
carousels
with my heart performing countless cartwheels,
when my words be trippin' on treadmills
while I'm with you, i don't even wanna stand still
but head over heels
fall
head over heels

we've told tales we'll stay in a hotel room
but really we be mixing each other's signals
wrapped in like a puzzling riddle,

couldn't figure if this love'll, solve itself but i'm
kinda dangerous
a little courageous
much more frivolous,

and when my head's spinning 'round like
carousels
with my heart performing countless cartwheels,
when my words be trippin' on treadmills
while I'm with you, i don't even wanna stand still
but fall
head over heels

Outrun

you can never speak the words you had

promised to keep

you can never swing your fists to close ones that

love you deep

you can try to outrun the life you lived,

but like you, like the trees,

they stay put where they're in

still continuing to grow,

you can never outrun getting old

each time you seek,

don't ever weep,

just so you know:

you reap what you sow

you're good turns to gold.

Shedding

you cut me so deep, while I was still bleeding
woke me from my sleep, while I was still
dreaming
you dug a hole in my heart, so why do you keep
on digging?
you lit my soul on fire, so why am I still
burning?

you called me on the phone, while i was alone
then
shattered my bones, while I was still broken
i'm hugging these walls, as my scars are under
an open ceiling
but you quit the fall, so higher than the given
healing

sealing my faith, that's shaking,
it's surging, wavering through the bleeding
but it's these teary streams, that do the easy
running

fire trapped lungs, in an empty shell

i'm shedding, i don't know how to feel

it's worse when one can't do their own imagining

Heartbreak colours of the sky

will i dream during the asking?
will i give up during the wishing?
every stoplight that runs the red
will be like my heart is escaping

how my light is changing colours
off of the sky, with flying kisses
gifted down onto you, oh i miss this,
and how we talked throughout the night

but i be wishing this trust was fully fixed like it
used too,
been seeing my cup is half empty, and yours is
half full,
you see pieces of my heart broke when you
decided to

leave me a long kiss underneath, a purple
moonlit scene

then i'd wake up with, only me in a sunrise

tangerine

before our love could grow into something good,

you leave me blue,

you leave too soon,

i wish we would stay evergreen

now that you caught me

dancing to the rhythm and singing the blues

and just like a fresh cut wound

you demanded to rip the blissful hues

off of the sky

we were close to being colours

yeah, they abandoned from my sky

now i'm lost without you,

you standing by my side

feels like i'm floating for nothing

feels like i'm hurting when loving

do i hide my life for those living?

and go onto something more fulfilling

Every

in every corner of my sky
you make constellations die

in every write, my hands scribe
the playful darkness of one's mind

oh i ask God
if I could
see the ending of this life
'cause i'm convinced the future lies

in every ocean it is trying
to make peace with the fire

in every picture i've memorised
you still make my heart cry

oh i ask God
if He could
turn every song into smiles
'cause letting you go hurts

Partly ghosted

you keep a monitor on me
keep a watchful eye, but can't see
how i'm under your radar, you beat
my soulful side, lost in the making

you're out to get under my skin
you tweak the score just to be free
too weak for war, you're 'ready winning
and I save the seas, that do the taking

Mad at love

i love the kind of love
when you love out loud
when he loves her openly, purely and proud

one for the taking
that love is kinda wild
never heart-breaking
that love is in the air
never suffocating

when the sudden laughter as we kiss
no better taste than his
laughter in my mouth
we keep these learning places
and lean into loving spaces

dream me the world
something new every night
she asked for that magic
and to never lose the fight

asked him to move in with her, that is in her
heart
so that he can choose to love her
every day

although it was encompassing,
as much as the love was deafening, quickening,
maddening and blinding
he realised he liked her
while she loved him

Ghost of my past

you say things like you're always right

and you couldn't blame me when i'd unwind

one for the taking, enjoy tonight

free for all, our bodies would fight

no, i don't recognise me

it's a different ghost i see,

yes when you are with me,

all you can do

is be the best version of you

you ever wonder? what girl you'll get in the

morning

the one with the mind of a storm

one without warning

or a spark, shock of lightning

no, i don't recognise me

it's a different ghost i see,

yes when you are with me,

oh all i can be

is the best version of me

Leap of faith

he found gold in me

worth the keeper

worth keeping

or

did he find something

that's cheaper

that's chipping

Getting played again

getting far from the living

yet afraid from my beginnings

i'd like to see myself walk in -

to the future and

give a toast to freedom

i know it's a moment to take in

is this what i was waiting for?

i let it out, but it's amusing to you

your hope is wanting to gift me to you

i know my faith is strong,

but i'm weak then,

allowing myself to count back your mistakes,

recount the times and ways i got played

i guess it's what i paid for.

Lost

lost in thoughts
since your kiss was a bliss
we took the risk
and left afloat,
adrift in a new abyss

lost in your eyes
led to this constance
by your lips
was fed by lies
thrifting on old tricks

found my twin flame
but burnt from the hurt
oh how i wish i didn't chase
you would have learnt (you never learn)
why i came and stayed (from your mistakes)

lost for words
here and now is all

i know your heart is stuck

to grow and mature

it pains me that you're still unsure

don't leave this lonely heart

'cause here and now is

all we know,

all i know

but why'd you have to go

light the fire within my soul?

i try to convince myself

why'd i need to let you go

Everything we had

we don't talk like we did before, bye-bye
it's nice you fell off the face of the Earth
you'd lie and say "i don't miss you nor her"
yeah it was like you didn't know my worth

no i don't hit up your phone no more
'cause you used to hate how i text and say "what
for"
well does it feel good to be all alone now?
thinking to myself, when will i know how

you haven't moved on, yeah the both of you two
we're hanging, yet her memories are dangling
around you

it hurts to feel we get attached
to temporary pasts
i wonder if that's the reason the passion
never lasts
how you moved on from me, just to get her back

after everything that we had
it hurts
when you'd say nothing to me
it leaves me to question:
"how is the other is doing?"
after what they've had with her

She

she had friends that were her skies

they walked on by

fading by the sunlight

she had exes that rolled their dice

they wore disguises

she fell for all surprises

those times were hard goodbyes

she had the courage to outrun the life

she was tied in,

that she was once married to

she tasted their fruits

they were rotting,

freed from the trap

she was caught in

and so she knows when to show

and when to let go

You're too important to lose

From sharing every minute detail of your life

with one another

To being unaware of one's milestones

Best friends grew apart

Yeah we deserve someone

Who believes they're too important to lose

Not loving me

I'm so weak

I'm so pathetic

I would have caused so much hurtin'

I'm so hurt,

Giving too much affection

You keep on runnin'

You keep expecting

For me to be the old me again

Feels so good

To delete your feelings

I'm so happy for me, given the lessons

Once you're close

I then see you leaving

Now I'm left wonderin'

Why I keep chasing

Boys that are bad story

Turn to my bad decisions

Yeah you're bad story, boy

You got my heart listening
over my head in

Thought,
You were the solution
But,
I'm still out here in my delusion
Oh,
When you come back with the truth and
Then,
Leave me out here bruisin'

I guess I'll stick to losing,
Over somebody that isn't for me,
That isn't choosing me
No more excuses
For someone who is
Not loving me

Thick and thin

reality checked in

can't really be ahead to think

when you're on my skin

from letting you in,

to letting you go

you were never really there in the end,

through thick and thin

Be careful.

you are never able to forget anyone,

you've been with,

and you can never replace anyone,

what is lost is lost.

Nowhere to run

our tortured touch

had torched my love

you poked the fun

i took the cut

no game of luck

we're scorched by sun

you poured for one

no cure, we're scarred

no score for us

you pulled the plug

you know we're done.

Heartache

what i've realised is that i,

can see you gave every little

and i tried,

to build an entire future with you in my mind

you're the last person that allows me to believe

in love,

best believe

it wasn't us i didn't give up on

it was us that i believed in

Your loss, not mine

but it was difficult to watch

you

love some-one else

watch you leave just to tell

me

and not to my face

that you lost interest

and had none to gain

but it was easy to find

myself

watch me lead my life just to tell

yourself

and to the mirror

why'd you quit my embrace

and witness

your error

A-N-S-W-E-R-S

why can't I gift wrap what you said
like a bouquet of flowers, i've not yet
dreamt of my life instead
i'm like your ballet dancer, yeah
floating and twirling 'round in your bed
before you hit the May showers, you set
a chance for me to write you ballads
so here's another ballad

do i want to be crushing?
this July, you made me question
first date when i'm gushing over you
"don't need to be rushing"
but fourth date, you're 'ready running
but i'm happy to be searching too

happily committing my love to you just to see
how you're treating your love to someone else,
not me
if you're cheating on love, baby
let it be me please

I'm A to the N-S-

take a good guess, W quick look, go back of the

book

E-R-S

pass the test, give it a rest or i'll give you my

answers soon

say yes to A to the N -S- W, E-R-S

believed it was all in my head

until I read all of it in bulls***

slept on lies, that were covered up, in between,

and underneath the bedsheets

even fell for that goodbye, now i'm over it)

left for me a spell,

even sung your love language,

i'll make it into a hit, yeah, I'll turn it into a hit

but I hate to be crushing you?

'cause June felt like I ruined it too

the sixth date, when I did the running

"I need to be trusting"

and seventh or eighth we could be f*ing

but I'm happy to be searching,

happily committing my love to you just to see
how you're treating your love to someone else,
not me
if you're cheating on love, baby
let it be me please

I'm A to the N-S-
take a good guess, W quick look, go back of the
book
E-R-S
pass the test, give it a rest or i'll give you my
answers soon
say yes to A to the N -S- W, E-R-S

will you be there for me baby, till next April?
cause i have all the answers still,
still take a wild guess of what we will be
be surprised of what's next, you'll see
see i'm your answer baby, please

Frozen

i didn't give up when
distance never breaks our bond
you said it was us then,
and not the connection we fought
for it was the surface level that never really
broke
it was the ending you wrote

i look around, other's lives moving,
had unanswered prayers, like what are we even
doing?

without you in this room, there's always here
and now
where will you be, what will i do when i'm
celebrating?
do i save it for later, or do it before then?

you left me broken
with the ending you had chosen

life continued on,

yet mine was still

frozen

love can last

if you don't wish it too well and fast

seen

i was so in love

that it didn't hurt me for you to leave

i don't feel heartbroken no more

i was just hoping

it'd be you and me in the end

;

you survived too many storms to be bothered by
raindrops.

A puzzled piece

we try to find the missing, puzzle piece

to fit into our lives,

but it ends up with what they took,

not what was missing

it was in the form of some memory

of you away with them,

locked in their brain, bottled deep within,

a puzzled piece, i am

to then go and find myself a new place

the try was never to complete the puzzle

but another try was made in order to find

another,

both of you not in the exact shape - but finally

the perfect fit to complete each other

Can we...

Laugh a little harder

Kiss a little stronger

Dance a little closer

Why don't you

Love a little softer

Cuddle me a little tighter

Stay a little longer

'Cause I don't want you to go

I wasn't finished loving you so

I love love

i love love

painful love

tender love

every bit of your love

love that stains

love that hurts

love that heals

love that you remember forever

and love that makes you forget

the only real truth in life

and reason being here

Not all for nothing

sometimes you fall, but only silently
sometimes you break, but really gently and
quietly
sometimes it aches, but momentarily
sometimes you wake up finally when life was
frozen and hard to breathe
oh sometimes it takes your all, but not all is for
nothing

sometimes I think I was born backwards
sometimes i think on sitting trains of things from
yesterday
sometimes it takes, sadness to know happiness
sometimes it takes, bitterness to know sweetness
oh sometimes it takes your all, but not all is for
nothing

Old school love

I've seen it on big screens and those loved-up
parts
Believed in those old movie scenes
Old type of love sh**
Perfect moment
Relieved to meet
Old school love
Kiss in the rain
Knew it was fate kind of sh**
I had that old school love,
Believed in that type of love
Holding hands and cuddling up to your chest
But she'll leave you for an old school love
'Cause she's read
All about that type of love
That leaves you red,
Fragile,
Delicate like an evening rose
'Cause i live for those
And want how our story to go
But that's just me, wishful thinking

Call me old fashioned

Call me "old fashioned"
But i'll take that old school love any day
And real quietly, you'd steal my heart away
Something 'bout the way
You sweep me of the feet
Daydreaming and found me thinking to
Lay my face and rest my cheek in

Call me old fashioned
But i'll take that old school love any day
Nothing wrong with passion
Wish for moments we had, were things we
couldn't contain
Of burning sensations,
We could see our differences, yet we couldn't
feel the same
But yes, my made up perceptions of wanting
more than what seemed good,
Made me leave,
Just to feel insane.

Bloom and thorn

girls are like roses

they can breathe

through the cracks

without relapse

girls can bloom and thorn

choose to bud than to mourn

inner power, flower not torn

their beauty not yet born

girls can dance through

snow storms and rainy season

even they'll put the fire in you

or freeze you then

girls will fall at your feet

when you drop to pick up

them roses

just to please them

4,3,2

now i don't want it die

like the flight of butterfly

wings in the pit of my stomach

but i don't wanna ask and say,

"why you're moving away"

but i do,

"still love you"

it makes me sigh

my neck was your sky,

wish i knew how not to-

put it like how you

did with the weight of words do

they usually hit

like a tonne of bricks

forget that purple stain hurt from those lips

i'd still forgive, still want you on my skin after

everything

'cause the clouded thought of you counts back 4,

3, 2,

"i still love you"

He loves me, she loves me not

Hands picking petals

Mind won't settle

She loves me,

She loves me not

The glint in your eyes

The hint of your smile

He loves me,

He loves me, he fought

For me

To pick up a shovel

To bury my thoughts

Love writes novels

But you never know what you love

'Til it's gone

Pick yourself up,

Breathe in heavy

Doubt raised poems

Words wrapped in thoughts

No he loves me,

He loves me lots

Faux leather

wanted it to last

wanted it to be genuine

nothing fake, and not imitated

fell for you fast

wanted it to be real in the end

even wore you as a fashion statement

does it matter if you were faux leather?

i'd still wear you through whatever weather

days that winds blew, and the nights gone cool

if i'd choose, i would've worn better

cause parts of you, and of us, would wither

yet in this weather,

i could barely see, i could still sink in deep

deeper into your

faux leather

i could barely touch

or feel my body rush

so light as a feather

oh if i worn, something better

oh, if i knew,

i wouldn't wear you

i wouldn't wear

faux leather

needed you to change

needed me to move on, though it hurts

up in flames for all those waterworks

when i fell for old ways

i needed you to be there 'til the very end

even if we were, young, broke and scared back

then

just say i matter to you now and forever

i doubt we would go through whatever weather

for i knew you, when the sun shone through

i wanted you in the end rather than never

but i never meant to bring out your colours after

and never meant to bring the weather down

or sink in deep

i couldn't see clearer

yeah it would be so much harder

to remember

that faux leather

with no fear,

just all in you

you and your,

faux leather

Weight of the world

for i

don't need the weight of the world on my

shoulders yet

lay it on the feet, i'd wait 'til I get older...

sort of

gotta get my entangled knots of thoughts sorted

but you took me by the hand,

wanting more handful of happy years

i'm in awe

how you handled it holding back tears

i still have lessons to learn, money to earn

i still have books to read before they get returned

i still have jokes unheard and reserved

for you

but i don't need the weight of the world

Trusting the process…

Right then and there,
When everything feels and goes right
The one thing becomes a mess
And shatters you 'til you feel helpless
Hopeless,
When the negative outweighs the positive
When you're suffocating from losing all the
oxygen

Everything needs to balance in life,
Everything that rises must fall
Suffering and pain, we disguise it all.
So travel light, and walk like living suitcases.
Don't carry yours or someone else's burden.

Yet we do feel human. We feel grateful and
become humble,
when beautiful things and moments can come
from the worst situations.

Lima

Passed by more people

Than she ever helped

Seen by two of her pupil,

Couldn't really be felt

Used to be close and to fill what is near, closing

All is known for mirrored things

Except for what she dealt

She needs to put her hand works to sleep

Rest easy on the mind, 'til then she repeats

A masterpiece while time progresses, she sings

She is a mantelpiece for flowers to be thrown

under her

Mental fatality

hanging on the edge of a cliff

future's got ahead of her

not thinking carefully, even when taking risks

it's what lies in front of her

she took what fell

down her well,

her uncontrolled gills

breathing and downing pills

a dead body

with no limbs

is like a journey

without destination

shores will speak

but waves still seek

to take a body of a young,

that's a lost soul, led a natural feed

to pearly white cheeks

hours upon hours rest,

turned bleak

not much soul left except an awful reek

A tragic story

why do i let myself to ruin songs

playing it over and over again

why did i place trust in my own tragic story

watered my memories with tears

in all hopes for tomorrow

that the garden for myself will grow

in need of arms to hold

i'm at my weakest

eyes see me at my lowest

and when a heart will love me at my worst

i'll find the one who leads me to love me first

Glow

aim to be framed to picture our perfects

could we blame it on society

study our own flaws to fracture our defects

where is the beauty in all of that?

concealer on, think it'll heal ya

'til the filter is gone, girl i feel ya

oh the anxiety took me higher than my heels

shadows live in me, colours confide in me still -

this morning, ive been mourning a river

that flows

as the sun's hitting, i'll be glistening like a river

i'll glow

we're scared to be scarred, it may harden our

hearts

then what's the use,

too smooth to hide with a bruise like that

puffy eyes tells truths, if popping pills help you,

there's more to life,

oh better to be kind to issues like that

'cause the show must go

on and on and on

or no?

they'll be listening,

but i'll be glistening

like a river

i'll glow

let me glow

When life complicates

we'll ride on

pull your wild horses

sail on

push your wind to our desired course

breathe in

stop to smell the roses

batter up

start to hit whatever life throws us

Special

i tend to believe that outside things just can't be
controlled
i refuse to let temporary people touch my mind,
body and soul
i tend to believe that someone will swoop in just
to show
but God is saving me for someone special and
raw

Pilot

Go prioritise your peace

Go protect your energy

You're the author of your dreams

Never allow a struggle leave

You to turn your sky to a ceiling

Oh you must believe

That there is always a way

When there's a willing

Twist your losses to lessons

Wish for more daily blessings

You're the gardener of your growth

Be loved

what's more to life than to feel loved?

what's more to a partner than his or her hug?

searching for more won't make you feel

satisfied,

when being content with what you already have

in your present life.

THE END

9 789363 315112